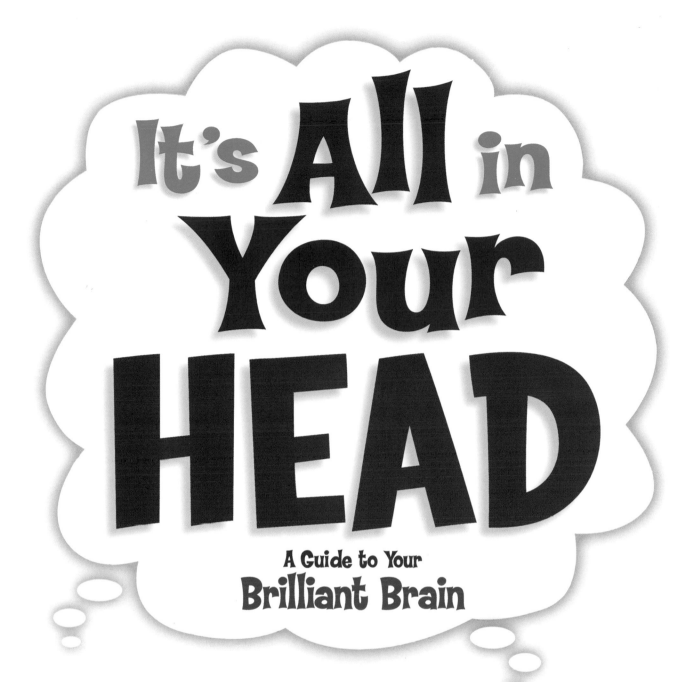

It's All in Your HEAD

A Guide to Your
Brilliant Brain

Sylvia Funston
Jay Ingram

Illustrated by Gary Clement

MAPLE
TREE
PRESS

Maple Tree Press Inc.
51 Front Street East, Suite 200, Toronto, Ontario M5E 1B3
www.mapletreepress.com

Distributed in Canada by Raincoast Books
9050 Shaughnessy Street, Vancouver, British Columbia V6P 6E5

Distributed in the United States by Publishers Group West
1700 Fourth Street, Berkeley, California 94710

Cataloguing in Publication Data
Funston, Sylvia
        It's all in your head : a guide to your brilliant brain / Sylvia Funston, Jay Ingram ; illustrated by Gary Clement.
— 2nd ed.

First published under title: a kid's guide to the brain.
Includes index.
ISBN 1-897066-43-0 (bound).—ISBN 1-897066-44-9 (pbk.)

Brain—Juvenile literature. 2. Psychology—Juvenile literature.
I. Ingram, Jay   II. Clement, Gary III. Title.

QP376.F86 2005   j612.8'2   C2005-900704-4

Design & art direction: Julia Naimska (interior), Claudia Dávila (cover)
Illustrations: Gary Clement

Photo Credits
pp. 8 K. Wothe/The Image Bank; 11 Art Foxall/Bernstein Associates Inc.; 15 (A) Bill Ivy; 15 (B and C) Robert and
Linda Mitchell; 16 Omikron/Photo Researchers; 18 Dr. George K. Peck; 19 Bill Ivy; 28 Tony Thomas; 32 Dick Haneda;
40, 42 Budget Book Service Inc., N.Y. (from *Mammoth™ Book of Fun & Games* by Richard B. Manchester ©1979
Hart Associates); 44 Zhir Virani/National Daycare Photographers; 50 Raichle/Petersen, Washington University, St. Louis;
54 Dr. Richard Haier/University of California, Irvine; 56 Dick Haneda

We acknowledge the financial support of the Canada Council for the Arts, the Ontario Arts Council,
the Government of Canada through the Book Publishing Industry Development Program (BPIDP), and
the Government of Ontario through the Ontario Media Development Corporation's Book Initiative for
our publishing activities.

Printed in China

A   B   C   D   E   F

CONTENTS

YOU ARE HERE

The human brain has been called the most complicated object in the entire universe. But you'd never know it to look at it. A full-sized, grown-up brain weighs only about 1.5 kg (a little over 3 lb.) and appears to be made of some sort of pinky-gray jelly.

But wait. Just imagine you could shrink so that you were a hundred thousand times smaller and could stand on the surface of the brain. You might notice that the footing is a little soft, but the astounding thing would be how different the surface would look to a miniature you.

You'd be able to see that the brain is made up of thousands and thousands of brain cells, packed tightly together, stretching away as far as you could see in every direction. If you could shine a light down into the upper layers of the brain, you'd see that those brain cells are arranged both in columns that go deep into the brain and in sheets that stack up like the layers of a cake. A closer look would reveal that every single brain cell branches, like a tree, and every branch is connected to many — even hundreds of — other cells and their branches.

As you stood there you would see the arteries and veins that crisscross the surface swell and contract as blood surges through them. And though you might not immediately be aware of it, the entire brain under your feet would be crackling with electricity. There'd be sudden electrical bursts, first here, then there, with each new thought.

All that electrical activity zapping around such a complex organization of cells might make you think that the brain works like a computer. But there is no computer that can do what the brain can do: think and imagine itself in space and time. The brain seems to come already equipped with some of its functions, just like programs "hard wired" into a computer. But a computer doesn't constantly reorganize itself, the way the brain does as it creates new information pathways each time it learns something.

Thinking, imagining, learning and planning all happen in the outermost layers of the brain. The rest of it takes care of many other important jobs, such as keeping your temperature just right or putting you to sleep and waking you up. Different parts of your brain can do these things — and much more — all at the same time without you even being aware of it. If you can't wait to see what all these different parts look like, take a peek at the back of the book.

So far no one has figured out how to shrink you down to see the brain at work, but you have the next best thing right in your hands. As you read this book, you'll take an explorer's trip through your own brain. You'll come across Brain Benders to exercise your thinking — in case some of them stump you, most of the answers are on page 63. And along the way, you'll be putting your own brain to work as it helps you to explore itself! Have a great trip!

SENSES

YOUR BRAIN SPENDS A LOT OF ITS TIME PIECING TOGETHER A picture of the world from your five senses: sight, smell, taste, sound and touch. It also decides which pieces of information that it receives are important enough for your attention. It's generally believed that your five senses feed into five distinct areas of your brain, each area dealing with only one sense. However, the discovery of brain cells that react to many senses all at once means that researchers are re-examining how we sense things.

In one experiment, for instance, blindfolded volunteers were taught for five days how to read the raised dot patterns of Braille. Brain scans showed that at first they used only their sense of touch to read the dots, but soon the vision center in their brains became involved too, even though there was nothing to see! Amazingly, when their vision centers were temporarily put out of action with a magnetic pulse, the volunteers had difficulty reading Braille using only their sense of touch. They had come to rely on using two senses to perform the task.

Perhaps our senses aren't quite as separate as we once thought. Can you taste a banana without smelling it or feeling its squishy texture in your mouth? No — all those sensations must work together before you get that recognizable "banana experience."

Eye Spy

Stop-action Sight
Blindness can result when the visual cortex — the visual area at the back of the brain — is injured. Gisela Leibold suffered damage to the parts of her visual cortex that pay attention to movement. As a result, she sees the world in "stop-action." When she pours a cup of tea, she sees a stream of tea frozen in midair. Then she sees a cup with a little tea in it, followed by more tea in the cup, then more, and suddenly there's tea all over the saucer and table. Gisela solved this problem by painting a line near the top of her teacup. When the tea covers the line, she stops pouring.

If you think your eyes are like cameras, you're in for a shock. Even a fully automatic camera is still primitive compared to your eye. A camera "takes it like it is." Your eyes do much more.

Watch the Birdie

When this photograph was taken, light bouncing off the bird entered the camera and fell on the surface of the film. Materials in the film reacted to the different levels of light and captured an image of the bird.

You have a kind of "film" at the back of each of your eyes, called your retina. Like camera film, it is sensitive to light, but that's where the similarity ends. As the image of the bird travels from your eyes to your brain, it is taken to pieces!

Your retina's light-sensitive cells are connected to many other kinds of cells, forming a sort of mini-computer in your eye. This "computer" chooses which parts of the picture to send on to your brain. It might ignore a background that never changes in favor of the edges and corners of things, especially if they're moving. It pays attention to anything that's new. It's a bit like you when you hold the TV channel changer: only a few things are worth watching.

Brain Bender
If there are twelve 1-cent stamps in a dozen, how many 2-cent stamps are there in a dozen?

• • •

Your eyeball computer sends all these bits and pieces of information about the bird by nerve signals all the way to the back of your brain. Here, different areas of the brain work on each feature of the bird's image. Colors are processed in one place, shape and depth in another. If the bird flaps its wings, still other areas pay attention to the movements it makes.

Then, in a mysterious way, all the pieces of the picture come together. It all happens so quickly that you are instantly aware that you are looking at a bird. So, in a way, you really do see out of the back of your head!

Seeing the Unseeable

If your eye was like a camera and recorded absolutely everything it saw, seeing would be like looking through a fence! The meshwork of vessels that supply blood to your retina lies *on top* of the cells that detect light. That means they leave a constant shadow on your retina, but in fact you never see them. That's because your retina pays no attention to things that don't change.

Try this
Make the blood vessels in your eyes visible. You'll need a small flashlight — a pen flashlight is ideal. Close your eyes and, without pressing, carefully place the bulb of the flashlight against the top of your closed eyelid. Move the flashlight back and forth as fast as you can over your eyelid, and your network of blood vessels will suddenly leap into view.

Ribbitt Eyes
You might think *your* eye is choosy about what it pays attention to, but a frog's eye ignores almost everything! So what exactly does it see? It notices small, dark, moving objects. (Hey, they could be yummy flies.) It also notices large shapes that loom into view then stop near it. (Hungry herons have a habit of doing this.) It pays attention to shadows that fall over it. (Who knows, the shadow could belong to any number of threatening animals.) And it sees the color blue. You might think that a frog would like the color green, but a frog's brain really prefers blue. There's a good reason for blue being a frog's favorite color. When danger looms, jumping towards a patch of blue, whether it's water or sky, will usually get the frog out of danger.

EYE TRICKS

LOOK AROUND THE ROOM, THEN LOOK AT THIS PAGE AGAIN. Is anything missing? No? Don't be too sure. You have a blind spot in each of your eyes — the place where the cable of your optic nerve leaves each eye on its way to your brain. But unless you use this special trick, you are never aware that you have a "hole" in your vision. Why? Your brain fills it in for you.

Out of Sight

Hold this page about half-an-arm's length away from your face and close or cover your left eye. With your right eye, look at the blue button. Keep staring at the blue button and move the page from left to right a little, or back and forth, until the red button disappears into your blind spot. Now try covering your right eye and making the blue button disappear. If you practise with the buttons, you might get good enough at finding your blind spot to make other things seem to disappear. When King Charles II of England got bored, he'd look around at his courtiers and lop off their heads with his blind spot!

BRAIN BENDER
What well-known
phrase do these two lines
represent?

ONCE
10 AM

• • •

Try this
With the book flat on a table, make one of the buttons disappear into your blind spot. Then place a pencil flat across the page and slide it towards the missing button until its tip disappears. Keep moving the pencil and eventually the tip will reappear on the other side. Does the pencil have a hole in it where your blind spot is? No. Even though part of the pencil is still in your blind spot, the pencil looks whole. It seems your brain repairs the hole in the pencil, filling in the bits it can't see.

On the Side

How's your peripheral vision? That's the ability to see things happening off to one side or another. Your peripheral vision has to do with the position of two different kinds of light-sensitive cells in your retina — rod cells and cone cells.

Great athletes, like hockey legend Wayne Gretzky, are able to see things they don't appear to be looking at — out of the corners of their eyes.

Try this

Find out just how little detail you see in the world around you, even though you probably think you take it all in with one glance. Sit in a chair, look straight ahead and ask your friend to hold a face card from a deck of cards off to one side of your face. You'll be able to see the card easily enough, but you'll have no idea which card it is. Why? Its image is falling on the outer edge of your retina, which is full of rod cells. Remember, rod cells don't see details well.

Ask your friend to move the card out in front of you, little by little. How far does it have to move before you can identify it? You'll recognize the card when its image falls on the cone cells near the middle of your retina. Cone cells are good at picking up details.

EYE TO EYE

A Blinking Mystery

Why doesn't the room go dark every time you blink? You blink about 15 times a minute, yet you never notice. On the other hand, if you switch the room lights off and on as quickly as you can, which is about as fast as you blink, you can't help but notice that the room gets dark. The answer to this mystery is found in the brain. Every time your brain signals your eyelid muscles to close, it also stops paying attention to your eyes for a moment. Because your brain switches off your vision, then a fraction of a second later switches it on again, you don't see the darkness.

YOUR EYES AND YOUR BRAIN WORK VERY CLOSELY TOGETHER TO make up what you see. But what you see depends not so much on what is entering your eye as on what your brain decides to pay attention to. To prove it, make a cat disappear just like the Cheshire Cat in *Alice in Wonderland*.

Try this

Stand in front of a cat, or something the same size, with a blank wall to your right. Hold a mirror in your left hand, and place it against your nose with the shiny side facing the blank wall. Turn the mirror slightly towards your right ear so that your right eye can see the blank wall in the mirror. Your brain is now receiving two different images — the cat from your left eye, and the blank wall in the mirror from your right eye.

Now, move your right hand up so that you can see it in the mirror. When your right eye sees your hand in the same spot as your left eye sees the cat, the cat — or parts of it — will suddenly disappear! Why? The sudden movement of your hand momentarily captures the attention of your brain. If you concentrate hard on the cat's mouth, with practice you can make its "smile" stay even if the rest of its face disappears.

Op-Tricks

Look at the drawing on the right: which black line is longer? The one on the right? Wrong. If you measure them, you'll see that they are exactly the same length. But even after you measure the lines, the illusion is so strong that you can't convince yourself that they are the same. The explanation is simple. If you were looking at the two lines and nothing else, you wouldn't be confused. But the rest of the drawing makes it look as if one line is close and one far away. So, even though the two images in your eyes are exactly the same length, the one on the right seems to be much farther away, and your brain is fooled into thinking that it must be longer.

Try this

Sit down with a friend and count the number of times he blinks in a minute. Then see if you can get an idea of the size of his pupils. Next, ask him to solve the Brain Bender below. While he's working on it watch his pupils, and count the number of times he blinks. If his brain is working hard, he should blink less and his pupils should grow bigger.

Giveaway Eyes

Next time you sit down to a favorite meal with your family or friends, take a good look at their eyes. If everyone's hungry, the pupils of their eyes — the dark circles inside the colored part — will expand when they see the food on their plates. (Unless it's broccoli or spinach, in which case they might suddenly shrink down to a pinpoint!) When you're interested in something you see, your pupils expand. When you're not interested, they contract.

Your eyes contain other clues to brain activity. The harder it is to figure out something, the bigger your pupils get — at least until you've solved the problem. And even blinking provides clues to what's going on in your brain. Most of the time, a blink means that your brain is pausing before it goes on to think about something else. You usually blink at the end of a sentence, at the end of a page or when you get the answer to a math problem.

BRAIN BENDER
Jack planted some magic beans that doubled in height every day. On the tenth day, the beanstalk was 20 m (66 ft.) high. On what day was it 10 m (33 ft.) high?

● ● ●

THE NOSE KNOWS

YOU DON'T RELY ON YOUR SENSE OF SMELL AS MUCH AS YOU DO on your eyesight, and your ability to smell isn't nearly as developed as it is in many other animals. But smells can get instant reactions out of you. Even thinking about ten-day-old socks can make you wrinkle your nose. In fact, most of your reactions to smells are bad — even the word *smell* usually means an unpleasant odor. So why be able to smell at all? Among other things, you count on smells to warn you if your food is spoiled or if something is burning.

The Way You Smell

Way up in the back of your nose is a patch of tissue that contains millions of special nerves. They put out little feelers called cilia into the liquid mucus that covers them. When you breathe in through your nose, chemicals in the air dissolve in the mucus and some of them come in contact with the cilia.

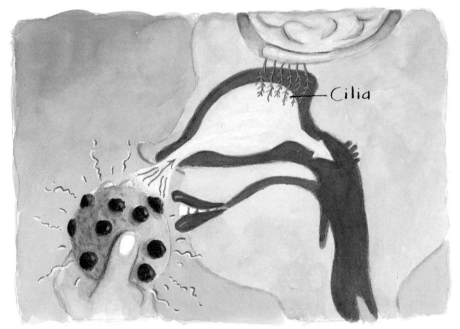

Smell Alert

Many animals use smell to warn others off their territory. Dogs urinate on trees to mark the boundaries of their property. When your cat rubs against you, it is marking you with scent from glands on its face. The Thomson's gazelle leaves a sticky black substance from a gland beneath its eye on twigs and leaves to warn away others. Only humans have to use fences and walls, doors and signs to say, "Keep away! This space is mine!"

Lots of Scents

You don't depend on your nose as much as other creatures do, but you still have an amazing ability to smell things. If you tried to make a list of all the smells you recognize, you might drop from exhaustion long before you finished it. The list might contain 10,000 different smells — everything from rotten eggs to grilled cheese sandwiches to campfire smoke and skunk. With a little training, you can do much better than that. People who make up new perfumes can tell the difference between odors that would seem exactly the same to you.

The surfaces of the cilia are studded with docking sites, which are specially shaped to catch the hundreds of different chemicals coming through your nose. Signals travel from the docking sites up your olfactory nerve directly to your brain, and arrive almost immediately at areas responsible for emotions and memories. Smells can arouse vivid emotions and reawaken long-lost memories . . . maybe because they can talk directly to these parts of your brain.

All the Better to Smell You With

Most of the brain cells you have as a kid are the cells you'll still have when you're 80. However, the cells that make up the nerves you smell with are constantly being replaced. If mice are exposed to new odors, they become more sensitive to them. This might be because they replace old, worn-out smell cells with new ones that are better tuned to the new smells. Perhaps this even explains why perfume experts can smell so much better than you can. They might have gradually acquired different smell-detecting cells.

Uncommon Scents

Below are three pictures and three descriptions of insects that use smell to survive. Can you match up each description with the correct picture? (Answers on page 63.)

(Answers on page 63.)

Try this
Pets know that no two people smell alike, but how far are *you* willing to go for science? Get four or five T-shirts that your family and friends have worn. Blindfold yourself and ask someone to hand you the shirts one at a time. Sniff each shirt and see if you can identify which belong to your family and which to your friends. Can you go further and identify which shirt belongs to each person?

1. This insect uses odor to mark a trail that its nest mates can follow to a source of food. The odor is so powerful, less than one-thousandth of a gram would make an odor trail all the way around the world!

2. The female of this insect releases tiny amounts of a chemical into the air when it is ready to mate. The scent, carried in the air, can attract males from kilometres away.

3. In a colony of these insects, one alone has an odor that ensures that it will continue to rule. If it stops producing this special smell, workers start feeding royal jelly to some of the young so that one of them will take over the rule of the colony.

TASTE TREAT

TASTE IS ONE SENSE THAT DEFINITELY RELIES HEAVILY ON ONE of the others: smell. You can prove how much smell determines taste the next time you have a bad cold. Wait until your nose is all stuffed up, then dig into one of your favorite foods. Can you smell it? Not a chance. Then can you taste it? Not likely.

Here's an even better way to prove that you can't taste what you can't smell. It's better because it gives you an excuse to buy a whole bunch of jelly beans and to eat them in the name of science.

Try this

You'll need a handful of different-flavored jelly beans and a friend who won't eat them all before you finish the experiment. Pinch your nostrils closed. Close your eyes so you can't see the color of the jelly bean you're getting, then ask your friend to pop one in your mouth. Still holding your nostrils closed, chew the jelly bean. Try to identify its flavor. Repeat this a few times, then let your friend do the experiment. Did either of you taste anything other than sweet? How about flavors: blackberry, licorice, mango or lemon? No, they all taste the same. That's because you can't smell them.

Time for more jelly beans! Try the experiment again, but this time don't pinch your nostrils closed.

BRAIN BENDER
Kim ate three slices of chocolate cake. Her father baked four chocolate cakes before eating two slices of chocolate cake. He cut each cake into eight slices. How many slices of cake were eaten?

• • •

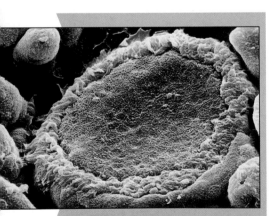

Budding Tastes

About 3,000 tastebuds, like this one, do your tasting for you, each one sitting at the bottom of a little pit in the surface of your tongue. As you chew your food, the chemicals from it dissolve in your saliva, and some of them wash into these pits and onto your tastebuds.

Ah! That's better. When you put the jelly bean into your mouth, it passes right underneath your nostrils and you smell a little bit of it. Then as soon as you bite into it, a gush of jelly bean odor rushes up from your mouth to the back of your nose. When you ate the jelly beans with your nostrils closed, you prevented any currents of air from entering your nose and carrying odors up to where your brain could smell them. No smell, no taste.

Yuck!

The bitterest substance in the world is denatonium saccharide. How bitter is it? All it takes is one drop of denatonium saccharide to make 3,000 1-L (1-qt.) bottles of soda pop taste absolutely awful.

Tongue in Cheek

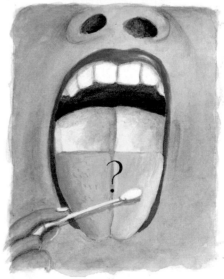

There are five tastes: sweet, sour, salty, bitter and umami (Japanese for delicious). Umami detects the yummy difference that glutamates — in particular MSG — make to flavors in food. Tastebuds in different areas of your tongue detect each taste.

Try this
The yellow section of the tongue on the right shows where you detect bitter tastes. To find out where you taste sweet things, sprinkle some crystals of sugar all over your tongue. Next, try for the more difficult sour and salty areas using first vinegar then salt. Hints: some of the taste areas overlap. Don't test MSG. And keep a glass of water handy for after each taste test. Check your findings on page 63.

Now Hear This!

THOSE TWO FLESHY THINGS THAT STICK OUT FROM THE SIDES OF your head — your ears — are only part of your complex hearing system. Most of the working parts are inside your head. In your ear canal, your eardrum is closest to the outside, and next to it are three tiny bones that vibrate every time it does. Behind these tiny bones is your snail-shaped inner ear, where sounds are changed to electric signals that travel to your brain.

But the part of your ear that you can see and feel, with all its funny twists and folds, plays an important role in how well you hear. It makes certain sounds seem louder and also helps you to locate where sounds are coming from.

A Faceful of Ear

A barn owl is much better than you at telling whether sounds come from above or below. Since it lacks outer ears, it collects sounds with its dish-shaped face. The feathery ruff on both sides of the owl's face funnels sounds to its ear canals, which are hidden beside its eyes. The amazing thing is that the left-side ruff is angled downward — good for catching sounds coming from below. The ruff is angled upward on the right, to catch sounds from above. With the ability to pinpoint exactly where mouse squeaks and rustles come from in the dark, it's no wonder the owl doesn't have to rely on its eyes to hunt!

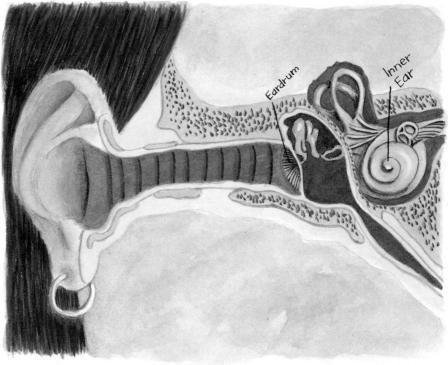

Right Hear

Being able to tell where sounds are coming from could mean the difference between life and death. The sound of a car behind you will make you jump onto the sidewalk fast! You're pretty good at telling how far to the left or the right a sound is coming from. Your brain figures it out by measuring the difference between the time the sound arrives at one ear and the time it arrives at the other. For instance, a sound coming from the right arrives at your right ear slightly before it does at your left.

Listen Up . . . or Down

You're not as good at telling whether a sound comes from above or below as you are at pinpointing it to the right or left, but you can still make a good guess. How? Somehow the weird loops and folds of your outer ear change sounds in such a way that your brain can tell whether they came from above or below.

Try this

How precise is your hearing? Make a big circle with several friends. One person sits in the center wearing a blindfold. Someone in the circle makes a short, sharp sound — a fingersnap, key jingle, mouth pop or whistle. The one in the middle has to point to exactly where the sound came from.

Try making the sound close to the floor, or high up, or try to make two identical sounds at the same time — one exactly in front and one behind. Can you improve your hearing by cupping your hands behind your ears? This makes sounds seem louder if you are facing them, but it might not help locate them.

Listen to Your Muscles

Just as your eyes have to ignore things that interfere with sight, so your ears have to ignore unimportant sounds — such as the sounds your own muscles make. Every time you move, the vibration of fibers in the muscles you use makes a low-pitched rumble. Normally you can't hear it because it's right at the bottom of the range of sounds you can hear, and your brain disregards it as unimportant. To the right is a trick that will let you listen in on your muscles.

A Stomachful of Ear
The praying mantis has a special ear on its underside that listens for only one sound: the hunting cry of a bat. As soon as that ear hears the bat, the mantis changes direction immediately, sometimes dodging, sometimes folding its wings and plummeting like a stone, to avoid being eaten.

Try this
Stick your fingers into your ears and listen carefully. Hear that deep background noise? Now, still keeping your fingers in your ears, squeeze your fists as tight as you can. The noise gets much louder. That's the sound of your muscles at work!

GOT THE TOUCH?

OW! YOU'VE JUST STUBBED YOUR BIG TOE ON THE LEG OF A chair and it hurts! But how does your brain know that it was a toe that you hurt and not your nose? Because running across the top of your brain like a hairband is your touch cortex, and it contains a touch map of your body. Nerve messages from your big toe travel directly to the big toe part of the map in your brain.

Introducing . . . Kidunculus

The scientific name for the body map that's stretched across your touch cortex is homunculus, which means "little man." But, since you're a kid, we're going to call it your "kidunculus." It's a strange sort of map. Some parts of the kidunculus body, such as the tongue and fingers, are much bigger than they should be in proportion to the rest of the body. It looks funny when you put it together, as you can see below. But it makes sense because some parts of your body are more sensitive to touch than others. These parts have more nerve connections than others. The more nerve connections a part has, the bigger it is on your kidunculus.

BRAIN BENDER
A man was out for a walk when it started to rain. He didn't have a hat or umbrella. His clothes got soaked but not a single hair on his head got wet. Why?

• • •

Try this

Figure out what your own kidunculus looks like, then draw it. All you need are two different-colored felt-tip pens (make sure the ink is non-toxic and will wash off your skin), a ruler, a piece of paper and a friend to help you. Do the experiment in a swimsuit.

Close your eyes and ask your friend to touch your skin with one of the pens just long enough to leave a mark. Then, without looking, try to touch exactly the same place with the other pen. Repeat this process all over your body. Measure how far off you were in each place, and keep a record. Use the record to draw your kidunculus.

You'll find that in some places your marks came very close to the ones your friend made. These areas have more nerves and should appear bigger on your kidunculus. For instance, if you came within 2 mm ($^1/_{16}$ in.) of the right spot on your finger, then draw big fingers on your kidunculus. But if you missed the spot on your calf by 2 cm ($^3/_4$ in.), draw a small lower leg on your kidunculus. If you are very precise, you'll find that your brain map exaggerates the size of your thumb until it's bigger than your entire trunk!

Monkeyunculus

Scientists have discovered recently that a touch map can change shape. The touch map changes in monkeys who spend two or three months spinning a little wheel with just one of their fingers. The finger that's been doing all the work starts to occupy a much bigger space on the map, and the fingers that have been idle have less brain map devoted to them.

This probably applies to humans too. No one has ever compared brain maps of soccer players and pianists, but the soccer player's homunculus probably has more space devoted to its feet, while the piano player's homunculus might have gigantic fingers!

BRAIN BENDER
Which is heavier:
a kilogram of feathers or
a kilogram of lead?

• • •

It's Mostly in Your Brain

Your kidunculus shows that touch goes on mostly in your brain, and it's like all your other senses: sometimes it can confuse or mislead you. One of the most amazing examples of this was discovered way back in 1846. Scientists are still not sure why this trick works.

Try this

You'll need three large coins of the same weight (the heavier the better), a glass of ice-water, a glass of water at room temperature, a glass of hot water (but not too hot to touch), a towel and a friend.

Drop a coin into each glass and let them sit for a minute. Quickly dry off one of the coins and ask your friend to drop her head back so that she can balance the coin on her forehead. While it sits there for about three seconds, quickly dry off another coin. Remove the first coin and replace it with the second. Repeat with the third coin.

Ask your friend whether all the coins were the same weight. Surprisingly, the cold coin will feel much heavier than the other two — some people say it feels four times heavier!

Next, repeat the experiment on your friend's forearm, near the elbow. The results are even more amazing. Not only will the cold coin feel heavier but so will the warm one. Now the room-temperature coin seems the lightest.

Most scientists agree that the nerves that transmit messages to your brain about pressure on your skin are also responsible for sending information about changes in temperature. When you put the cold coin on your friend's forehead, the skin there feels sudden changes in both weight and temperature, and the two messages get confused. But why this illusion works differently on different parts of your body is still a mystery.

The Phantom Hand

Sometimes when people lose an arm or a leg, they can still feel the missing limb! The reason is a mystery. In one case a doctor asked his patient to hold a coffee cup with his missing hand. As the patient thought he was grabbing the cup, the doctor suddenly moved it, and the patient yelled. He could feel the pain when the doctor snatched the cup from the hand he was holding it with . . . his phantom hand!

EMOTIONS

HOW ARE YOU FEELING RIGHT NOW? HAPPY? THAT'S GOOD. IT'S difficult to tell for sure, but there is evidence that it's the front left part of your brain that's responsible for holding your confident, happy feelings while the front right part of your brain is the home of your unhappy feelings. But these aren't the only parts of your brain that work on your emotions. All your feelings are triggered and processed by an "emotion network" that hooks together many different areas of your brain.

Scientists know most about what happens in your brain when you feel afraid. That's because they've been able to trace fear messages traveling around the emotion network. Some of your other emotions, such as sadness or joy, are more difficult to trace. In fact, not much is known about them at all!

Unless you're a skilled actor, you advertise every emotion that your brain triggers. How? Through your body language. Learning what facial expressions, body positions and gestures mean will help you understand people better because you'll know what they're feeling — no matter what they say.

THE FRIGHT STUFF

You stumble onto the stage, heart pounding and knees trembling, your mouth as dry as sawdust. Facing your audience, you take a deep breath and hope desperately that when you open your mouth to speak, something besides a terrified squeak will come out.

You are in the grip of a powerful emotion — fear. In this case, you are experiencing what scientists call "learned fear." Having lines to speak in a play doesn't threaten your safety. But you have learned from experience that being stared at by hundreds of people can *feel* threatening.

The place where you learn to be afraid of situations like this is deep inside your brain, in two structures that look like fat almonds. These structures are called amygdalas, and it seems they are able to link emotions to memories, good and bad. If you ever burned your fingers on a hot stove, it's your amygdalas you've got to thank for never wanting to do it again.

BRAIN BENDER
Which set of letters doesn't fit, and why?
NOPQ   HIJK
CDFG   UVWX   QRST
● ● ●

24

Scared Stiff

After your brain receives the information from your senses that you are in a threatening situation, chemical messages zap around your emotion network. Within two seconds, here's what happens:

• Your heart rate and blood pressure increase.
• Your digestion slows.
• Blood moves from your skin and digestive system to your brain and muscles, where it is most needed.
• Your lungs expand so that you can take in more oxygen.
• Your pupils enlarge to let in more light to help you see better.
• Your sweat glands work overtime to cool your body more efficiently in case you have to run away, or stay and fight.

What Are You Afraid Of?

Are you scared of getting peanut butter stuck to the roof of your mouth? Then you're suffering from a phobia, an ongoing, unreasonable fear of something. It's thought that phobias develop when something makes you remember unpleasant experiences from long ago. This mixed-up list shows phobias and their names in the wrong order. Can you match them up? (Answers on page 63.)

Bite or Flight?
The amygdalas help all warm-blooded animals to survive by triggering their "fight or flight" response. A rat whose amygdalas have been removed loses its fear of cats because it no longer remembers that they are its enemies. In one experiment, a fearless rat walked straight up to a sleeping cat and nibbled on its ear!

Phobia Name Game

What do you feel?
1. Fear of injections
2. Fear of storms
3. Fear of enclosed spaces
4. Fear of water
5. Fear of computers
6. Fear of learning
7. Fear of getting peanut butter stuck to the roof of your mouth

What is it called?
A. Claustrophobia
B. Arachibutyrophobia
C. Belonephobia
D. Logizomechanophobia
E. Astraphobia
F. Hydrophobia
G. Sophophobia

$$xy \pm (2 \times \sqrt{127}) \, \Sigma qb$$
$$27,000,000^3$$

FEELING FINE

IN A WAY, YOU HAVE THREE BRAINS IN ONE. THINK OF THEM AS your reptilian, feeling and thinking brains. The three developed at different times over many millions of years, and they sit one inside the other, with your thinking brain — the last to develop — on the outside. Your three brains talk to each other constantly, and special areas in each brain are "wired" together to form an emotion network. The messages that zip around this network trigger the emotions you feel and your response to them.

Feeling Brain

Your feeling brain, or limbic system, evolved after the reptilian brain, but only in warm-blooded animals. It controls your body temperature and all your emotions, and works with your thinking brain for some forms of learning and memory.

Thinking Brain

The outer covering of your thinking brain is the cortex. This most recent part of your brain sets you apart from other creatures. The front of your thinking brain decides how strong a reaction should be to messages from your feeling brain.

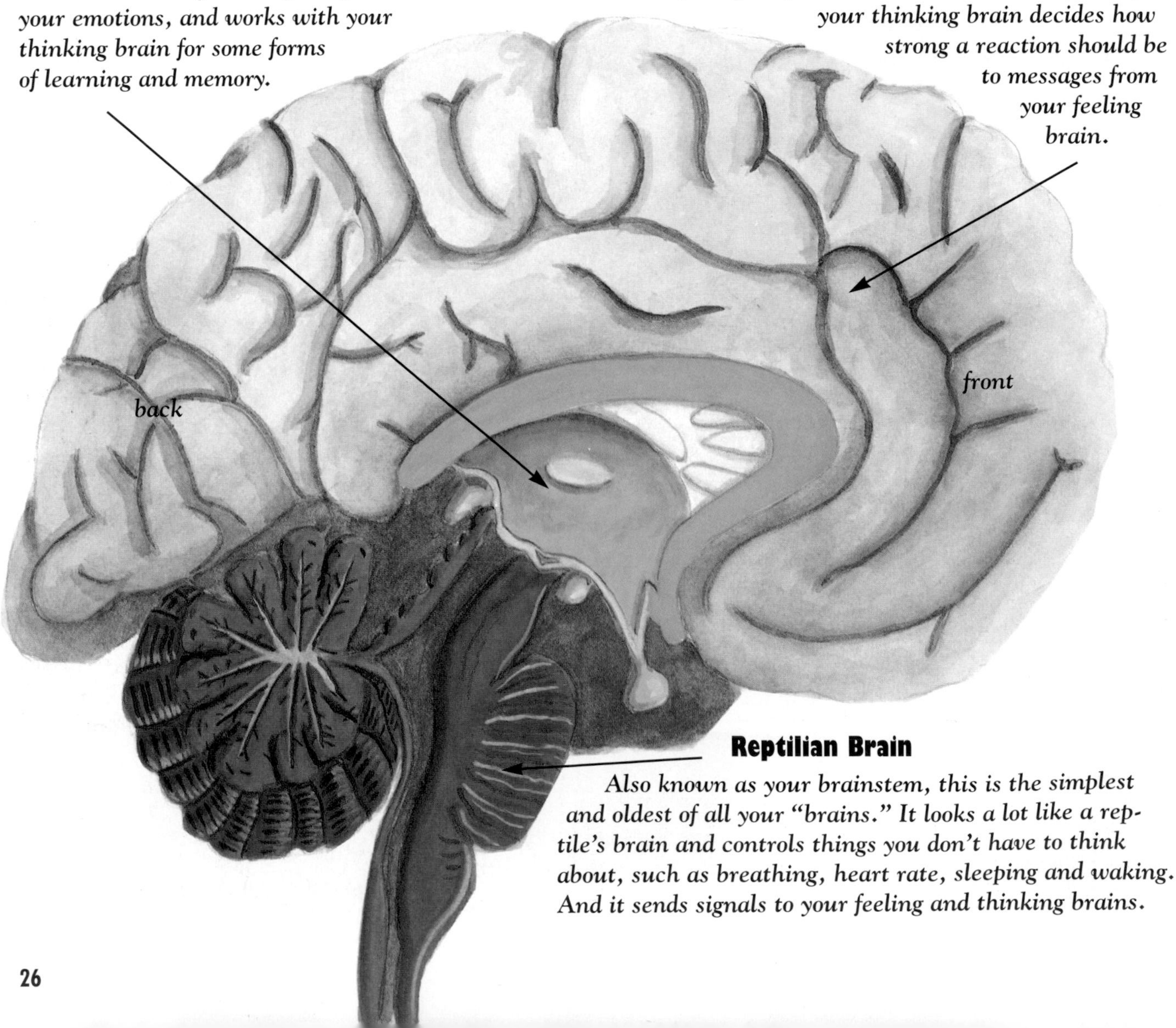

back

front

Reptilian Brain

Also known as your brainstem, this is the simplest and oldest of all your "brains." It looks a lot like a reptile's brain and controls things you don't have to think about, such as breathing, heart rate, sleeping and waking. And it sends signals to your feeling and thinking brains.

Mood Food

Did you know that what you eat affects your moods? Here are two situations and some foods that will improve the way you feel. But which foods will help you in which situation?

1. It's the first class after lunch and you're feeling sleepy. What should you have eaten at lunch to help you stay alert?

2. You're so angry you could burst. What should you eat to help you calm down?

If you chose proteins for alertness and carbohydrates to calm you down, you're absolutely right! High-protein, low-fat foods such as fish and skim milk contain an amino acid that your brain changes into chemical messengers that zap around saying, "Wake up, pay attention!" . . . and you do! Carbohydrates such as apples or bagels contain a different amino acid that your brain changes into chemical messengers that spread the word, "Calm down" . . . and guess what? You do.

You can confuse your brain by eating a candy bar that's a mixture of carbohydrates (sugar, chocolate or caramel) and proteins (nuts). It won't know whether to calm you down or wake you up!

Bye Bye, Happiness

Phineas Gage was only 25 years old in 1848 when a long metal rod was driven through his head by an explosion. It completely removed the front left part of his brain — the part that is thought to control good feelings. The loss of the front left lobe of Phineas's brain destroyed a vital part of his emotion network and important centers that helped him control his behavior. He changed from a hard-working, likable fellow into an impulsive, loud-mouthed, bad-tempered man. In fact, his accident put him into a bad mood that lasted the rest of his life.

Turn a Bull into a Pussy Cat

Jose Delgado thought he knew where to locate the brain's pleasure center, and he chose a dangerous way to demonstrate it. First he implanted an electrode into the feeling brain, or limbic system, of an aggressive fighting bull. Then he stepped into the ring with the bull. The bull charged. Delgado pushed a button, the electrode fired — and the bull stopped in its tracks! Raging meanie one second, sweet as pie the next. Luckily for Delgado, he had put the electrode in just the right place: the part of the bull's feeling brain that causes intense pleasure.

27

FACE FACTS

<small>PUT A PAPER BAG OVER YOUR HEAD, STAND UP STRAIGHT AND,</small> unless you're shaking in your shoes, people won't know what you're feeling. As soon as you remove the bag and start to move, however, your "body language" gives you away.

It's Written All Over Your Face

No matter where you go, most people will be able to recognize at least six emotions on your face, because people express them the same way all over the world. They are: fear, anger, happiness, sadness, surprise and disgust. Some scientists believe that these six emotions became fixed features of our feeling brains during our evolution — a bit like the wiring in a computer. One of the reasons they think this is that people who are born blind produce exactly the same facial expressions as people who can see.

Culture also plays a role in how you express emotions. For instance, if you live in North America or Britain you can likely put on a "smug" face — an odd mixture of a happy and an angry face — which people in other cultures might not recognize.

Try this
Can *you* identify each of the six emotions in these photos? (Answers on page 63.)

28

To Tell the Truth

One of these kids broke a vase, but both deny it. Can you decide which of the two isn't telling the truth? (Answer on page 63.)

Need a clue? Look at their eyebrows. If they're turned up slightly near the nose, there's a good chance that person is lying. Other signs of lying? Blinking a lot, blushing or not being able to look you in the eye. But be careful when you're reading these signs. In some cultures, it's rude to look someone in the eye, and people avoid doing it. Better stick to the eyebrow clue. You have to be fast to catch it, but it seems to work no matter who you're dealing with.

Two-Faced

A trained observer can detect a forced smile. How? A genuine smile is just as strong on both sides of your face, but a false one is usually stronger on the left side of your face. As well, a spontaneous smile makes wrinkles appear around your eyes, which don't show during a forced smile.

Try this
To find out if a pretend smile is stronger on the left side of your face than the right, you'll need two mirrors.

1. Put one mirror shiny side up on the table.
2. Stand the second mirror at right angles to the first with its shiny side to the right.
3. Rest the middle of your nose on the upright mirror, as shown. Look at the face you see and smile. The image you see will be made up of two right sides of your face.
4. Turn the upright mirror around so you can see the left side of your face and repeat step 3.

How different were the two sides of your face?

Could You Win an Oscar?
Two sets of nerves run from your brain to your face to produce facial expressions. One set you can't control, the other you can. If you stub your toe, the nerves you can't control will make you grimace. But if you're taking part in the school play and you have to pretend to stub your toe, you can make a grimace appear on your face by controlling the other set of nerves. The more control you have over this second set of nerves, the more you're able to disguise your true feelings.

BODY TALK

IF YOU THINK IT'S TOUGH KEEPING YOUR FACE UNDER CONTROL in an emotional situation, try controlling all the messages your body sends out about your true feelings. Here are four situations where someone is saying one thing but obviously feeling another. What should each person really be saying? (Answers on page 63.)

Sign Language

People who are hearing-impaired use special languages made up of movements. We all "sign" to express things without saying them. But be careful! A gesture that means one thing to you might mean something entirely different to someone from another country. Of the gestures shown below, two mean "yes," two mean "no," one means "come here" and the other means "goodbye." But which means which in these countries? (Answers on page 63.)

(Answers on page 63.)

Instant Attraction

Ever wonder why you're more attracted to some people than to others? Scientists think it might have something to do with two chemical messengers made in your brain. When you meet someone you think is attractive, both these messengers are produced in large quantities and they activate the pleasure center in your feeling brain. So just seeing that person actually makes you feel good.

BRAIN BENDER
A man doesn't have his driver's license with him. He fails to stop at a railway crossing, ignores a stop sign and travels three blocks in the wrong direction down a one-way street. A police officer watches all this but doesn't arrest him. Why?

• • •

Try this

Looking for something fun to do with your family or friends on a wet afternoon? Try to get through an hour without saying a single word. During this silent time, you have to "tell" each other things about yourselves — using body language only.

Fuzzy Feelings

How do we know whether animals have feelings? In the case of a gorilla called Koko, scientists were able to ask her because she had learned to communicate using American Sign Language (ASL). When Koko's pet cat All Ball died suddenly, Koko acted as if she were grief stricken, and was able to tell her human friends how sad she felt. The three animals below don't need ASL to let you know what they are saying. Can you read their body language? (Answers on page 63.)

Cold-blooded or Hot-blooded

Don't ever expect your pet turtle to greet you with a smile on its face. A turtle doesn't show emotions because it doesn't feel them. Cold-blooded creatures like reptiles, amphibians and fish lack both a feeling brain and a thinking brain. So your pet turtle, snake, goldfish or lizard will never mope around when you go to school or jump for joy when you come home.

Your pet dog does have a feeling brain and a thinking brain. But does this mean that when she wags her tail she feels happiness in the same way that you do? It's difficult to know. One reason *you* experience such a rich range of emotions is that your feeling brain is linked directly to your thinking brain. And your thinking brain is gigantic compared with that of your dog.

The direct connection between your feeling brain and your thinking brain is also why you can get emotional over an idea or a memory. If you've ever felt jealous at the thought of someone you really like wanting to spend time with someone else instead of you, you know how painful some ideas can be. And memories are something else again.

BRAIN BENDER
John was asked how many pets he had. He replied: "They're all cats but two, all dogs but two and all goldfish but two." How many pets does he have?

• • •

32

MEMORY

PUT YOUR HAND ON YOUR FOREHEAD WHILE YOU'RE READING this page. Why? Because directly beneath it is the part of your brain that allows you to remember the words you're reading long enough to understand a complete sentence. Without your working memory, which operates in the front of your thinking brain, you'd forget the first words in this sentence before you got to the end.

Your working memory works fast. It can retrieve stored memories instantly as it links up one thought to the next. And you also have other types of memory systems that allow you to remember for longer periods. You're about to meet these systems. At the same time, you will find out how you recognize faces, how you can improve your memory, even how animals use their memories. And you'll solve the mystery of why you can't remember anything from when you were a baby.

REMEMBER THIS!

BRAIN BENDER
What would you be looking at if you saw this combination of letters and a number?
WXY 9

• • •

REMEMBER YOUR FAVORITE BIRTHDAY PARTY? OKAY . . . WHAT IF that memory went like this — you've just blown out the candles on your cake. Suddenly you trip and fall . . . straight into the cake! Mmmmm, chocolate. How and where would your brain store that memory? And how would you recall it, even if you didn't want to?

The Memory Bank

Memories are stored and retrieved by two special parts of your brain. Your wishbone-shaped hippocampus, right in the middle of your feeling brain, is responsible for filing similar memories together in the right place. The outermost part of your thinking brain, the cortex, fits in a many-folded layer over your whole brain, and has the job of finding those memories when you want them.

Hide and Seek

When you fell face forward into your birthday cake, your hippocampus suddenly got very busy. It filed the memory of the color of your mom's face and the stain on your new clothes in your visual cortex at the back of your head, together with all your other visual memories of the colors red and brown. It tucked away the smell of the cake with other chocolate smell memories just behind your nose. It sent the shrieks, gasps and giggles to your hearing cortex on both sides of your head. And it stored the feel of the cake with similar sticky sensations in the thin strip of touch cortex that runs across the top of your brain.

You recall this sticky moment when your cortex, or thinking brain, turns on all these bits and pieces of memories. It's as if you're experiencing your birthday cake demolition party all over again — whether you want to or not. But how does your cortex sort through your stored memories, all at the same time, and instantly come up with just the right ones that make up the memory you're looking for? That's still a mystery.

Memory Lanes

Every time you learn something new, such as the name of a new friend, some of the connections between your billions of brain cells change. What this means is that your brain isn't hard-wired like a computer. Instead, each time you learn something, your brain creates new memory pathways by reorganizing the way your brain cells connect to each other. The more you learn, the more your brain changes.

Try this
How many new memory pathways can you create in your brain by finding new meanings and associations for words? As you can see in the illustration above, the word *box* has at least three different associations: a box is a square container; to box is to engage in the sport of fighting with gloves; a box kite is shaped like a box.

Make up a list of words and see how many associations you can find for them. Challenge your friends to come up with more.

BRAIN BENDER
Quick! You have one minute to come up with a word that begins with the letter M in each of the following categories:

TOWNS
OCCUPATIONS
FOOD
CLOTHING
MOVIE STARS
MUSIC
FLOWERS
BIRDS
WET THINGS
DRY THINGS
SPACE OBJECTS

• • •

Remember Your Friends
When you phone a friend, do you see her face in your "mind's eye"? If so, you are experiencing your amygdalas at work. Remember them from the chapter on emotions? They're the part of your feeling brain that linked up memory and fear to produce a bad case of stage fright. This time, however, your amygdalas are linking up pleasant memories — the memory of your friend's voice with the memory of her face. You've probably figured out by now that your feeling brain not only plays a major role in your emotional life, it also helps you to store and recall memories.

MEMORY WORKS

Try this memory test
Look at this list for one minute. Try to remember the items on it. You'll find out how well you've done later.

YOUR WORKING MEMORY COMBINES YOUR MOMENT-TO-MOMENT awareness with instant recall of stored information. It lasts long enough for you to do a carry-over operation in your head while adding numbers, or to remember which fingers are supposed to strike which keys when you're playing a memorized piece on the piano. But it's not the only memory system that you have.

Short-term memory lasts for about 30 seconds — that's long enough to dial a telephone number you've just looked up. If the telephone number is important and you keep repeating it to yourself, eventually it will be stored in your long-term memory. Not everything makes it into long-term memory — as you might find out if you're not prepared for a test at school — but once memories are stored in your long-term memory, for the rest of your life they can resurface whether you want them to or not.

Eggs
Rhubarb
Steak
Butter
Toothpaste
Watermelon
Shoelaces
Spaghetti
Cauliflower
Apples

LONG-TERM MEMORY

SHORT-TERM MEMORY

The Man with No Past

People who have lost parts of their memories help researchers determine what kinds of memories we have. For example, K.C. is a young man who suffered brain damage that resulted in amnesia, or memory loss. K.C. cannot remember anything he has done or experienced in his past — and that includes things he did or people he met just a few minutes before. But K.C. can recall other kinds of memories, such as facts he learned in school, and how to ride a bike and play the piano. He can even draw a map to show how to get to his family's summer cottage — although he can't remember ever being there! What K.C.'s unusual form of amnesia proves is that we have one kind of memory for facts and skills, and another kind for personal events.

The Short and the Long of It

Give your short- and long-term memories a workout, and see how well they do. Start with your short-term memory.

Try this
Look at this list of words for 10 seconds, then cover the page and try to recall them.

CAT RED SIT PEN HOT

Now look at this list of words for 20 seconds, then cover the page and try to recall them.

DOG HOP SIP RUN CAN LIP MAT NIP FUN TAP

Don't worry if you couldn't remember all the words in the longer list. Short-term memory span is quite limited. It's good for carrying between five and seven words, colors, geometrical designs or numbers. That's part of the reason why your telephone number is only seven digits long.

Now try your long-term storage ability.

Try this
Here's a nonsense rhyme for you to memorize.

"As I was going up the stairs,
I met a man who wasn't there.
He wasn't there again today.
Oh, how I wish he'd go away!"

Store this nonsense rhyme in your long-term memory. It will help if you return to it from time to time, and repeat it until you've got it word perfect.

Chickadees and Hippos
Black-capped chickadees don't fly south for the winter, so each autumn they store as many as 200 tasty tidbits a day under leaves and in tiny cracks in tree bark. Months later they can return unerringly to their secret food stashes.

A Toronto scientist suspected that chickadees rely on their memory rather than their sense of smell to find the food. To prove it, he released chickadees that had no hippocampi into a small, artificial forest where they'd hidden their food. He was right! The chickadees flew here and there, unable to remember where they'd hidden the seeds.

In a later experiment, the same scientist discovered that, of 23 kinds of North American birds, those that stored food all had bigger hippocampi than those that flew south for the winter.

PLACE THE FACE

IF YOU LIVE ALL YOUR LIFE IN A BIG CITY, YOU SEE MILLIONS OF faces, no two of them exactly alike. Amazingly, over time you'd be able to recognize thousands of them! How is this possible?

Psychologists experiment to find out exactly how we recognize faces. Sometimes the hairline, eyebrows and eyes seem to play a bigger role in face recognition than noses and mouths, other times prominent features seem to spark memory, while at still other times overall impression seems most important. It might be that we use different ways of recognizing faces, depending on the circumstances. Try these experiments and decide for yourself.

Those Lips, Those Eyes

Do you think that Superman's glasses and change of hairstyle make a better disguise than Batman's cowl and mask? Or should both superheroes wear a funny nose and moustache?

Try This

Cut out magazine photos of four famous people. Show them to someone else, after you've made each one look like one of these illustrations: upside down; the top half cut off; the bottom half cut off; the hair, eyes and eyebrows gone. Which faces were easy to recognize?

If the third photo was easy, you've proven what most studies show: the top part of a face is easier to recognize than the bottom. With the first photo, it depends on a person's age. Why? People younger than about 14 can recognize upside-down faces better than older people can. Another study showed that the last photo should be difficult. It's missing what was mentioned most by people who were asked to describe photos of faces: hair, eyes and eyebrows.

Flash Recognition

Look at the face to the right. Have you seen it before? Turn back to page 28. Yes, it's the same face, but this time you're seeing it as a caricature, a drawing with some of the features exaggerated.

Did you get a flash of recognition from the caricature? A recent experiment used life-like drawings and caricatures to study this sort of recognition. Students looked at drawings of faces made from a police identi-kit, and later recognized the faces with more certainty from *caricatures* rather than from the original drawings.

Do you get a flash recognition of a caricature because your brain remembers faces that way? It might be that your brain picks out prominent features and exaggerates them in your memory to help distinguish one face from all the others you've seen.

BRAIN BENDERS
How many months of the year have 28 days?

Say the months of the year in alphabetical order.

● ● ●

Look-alikes

Believe it or not, when you first see twins you instantly memorize one face before looking at the other. If the second face matches your memory of the first — if you recognize it — you decide that the twins are look-alikes. But how do you compare their faces?

A magazine called *Spy* used to feature photographs of famous people who looked so alike they might have been twins separated at birth. Psychologists used these "Separated at Birth" photos to test how we compare faces. The test group decided several pairs of photos showed look-alikes when they didn't have to think about why. But when they compared the photos feature by feature, they didn't find much similarity at all! This seems to show that the brain stores an overall impression of a face rather than separate features. It uses this overall impression to decide if one face resembles another.

Try this
Do you know people who look a lot alike? If they are famous or just people you know, all you need is a photograph of each person to do the "Separated at Birth" experiment yourself.
1. At your first glance at the photos, do you think the two people look similar?
2. Now, spend some time studying and comparing their individual features: look at the eyes, the noses, the mouths, etc. Do you still think they look similar?

YOUR MIND'S EYE

CAN YOU IMAGINE WHAT IT WOULD BE LIKE IF YOU COULD NEVER forget anything you'd ever seen? Imagine how easy school work would be. But if you could never forget anything, how could you prevent earlier memories from interfering with later ones?

Take a Picture

A Russian man named Shereshevsky had an incredible memory that he proved as a stage performer, two shows a night. The audience called out long lists of numbers that he would write down and then later recite perfectly from memory. But he began to worry that the first set of numbers would pop into his mind during the second show, so he imagined crumpling up and then burning the first sheet of numbers to make sure he'd forget the numbers written there!

Some people have what is known as a photographic memory. One out of every ten people are born with one, but most of them lose it by the time they're adults. Usually, it happens around your age. But don't despair! Even if you don't have a photographic memory, you can strengthen your visual memory through practice.

Try this
Look at these 12 designs for 30 seconds. Got them? When you get to page 42, you can see how many you're able to recognize.

Try this

Examine the scene below for 30 seconds. Do it slowly and systematically. In your imagination, divide the scene into a grid made up of squares. Start at the top right of the picture and move your eyes slowly from side to side, then from top to bottom, covering the entire grid.

Now, cover up the picture and answer these questions.

1. What is the name of the boutique?
2. Name at least six things being held by people.
3. How many wheels are in the picture?

Don't be discouraged if your answers didn't match up with the picture, just repeat this experiment later in the day. How well can you remember other details? Did you improve with practice? Bet you did!

Flashbulb Memories

If you've ever witnessed or heard about a very important event that was either truly great or extremely tragic, chances are you can remember it very clearly — when and where you were when it happened, how old you were and who was with you. This kind of strong, picture-clear memory is known as a flashbulb memory.

You remember a flashbulb memory so well because the event was important to you, and also because you tell and retell its story so many times. But just because you remember it well doesn't mean your memory of it is accurate! By listening to other people's accounts of the event or seeing it on TV, you keep adding fresh details to your own memory. Eventually your own memory changes to include other people's memories of the same event.

Are You My Mother?
How do animals remember and recognize each other? Many use smell and sound to identify others of their own species. But some animals lack ways to recognize each other. Baby songbirds don't seem to remember their parents at all. In fact, an elephant could visit their nest and, as long as it brought them food, they wouldn't care! In general, it seems that animals that live in groups — such as wolves, gorillas and us — recognize each other by their faces.

MEMORY BOOSTERS

Try this

How many of the designs below do you remember seeing on page 40? Write down the numbers of the designs that look familiar. (Answers on page 63.) Most people find that it's easier to recall pictures than to remember words or numbers.

HOW CAN YOU IMPROVE YOUR MEMORY? PEOPLE HAVE BEEN asking that question for thousands of years. In fact, it was a poet in ancient Greece, named Simonides, who came up with one of the best memory aids ever invented.

Simonides' House

Remember the shopping list we asked you to memorize on page 36? Write down all the items you can remember. How many did you get? Good old Simonides would have remembered all ten. Here's his secret. He would take an imaginary walk through a building he knew. Then he'd place items from the shopping list in silly places. Take a walk through the house below and you'll find all the items on the shopping list. Think of each item and connect it to the place it's in. Cover the picture and imagine walking through the house again. Write down every item that you pass on your walk. Now you've got it! You can thank Simonides for your success.

Stick It

Here are a couple of quick tricks to help you make sure that facts will "stick" in your memory.

1. Take the initial letters from a list of things you want to remember and use them to make up a nonsense phrase. Like this — to remember the order of the planets from the sun (Mercury, Venus, Earth, Mars, Jupiter, Saturn, Uranus, Neptune and Pluto), memorize the phrase *Mother Very Early Made Jelly Sandwiches Under Nellie's Picture*. After 2019, when Neptune and Pluto switch places again, remember to change *Nellie's Picture to Paul's Nose!*

2. It's easier to remember facts if you put them into sentences that rhyme. Bet you'll always remember that stalactites are the ones that grow down from cave ceilings if you memorize this rhyme:

> *"Poor little stalactite*
> *Spends its days clinging tight."*

Memory aids like these are called mnemonic devices and, believe it or not, they really work.

By the way, how's your long-term memory for the rhyme you read on page 37? Keep trying to make it stick!

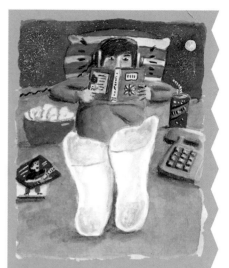

Ace a Test

Do you study late into the night listening to music and taking snack breaks every page or so? That strategy will get you great marks . . . but only if your teacher plans a test at midnight with rock 'n' roll and snacks. Otherwise, it's a good idea to study during the day in a quiet room with no distractions. Even better, see if you can spend some study time in the room where you will be tested at roughly the same hour as the test will be held.

How does this work? Your brain processes and stores memories differently depending on how you feel and what's happening around you. The secret of your study plan is to match how you feel when you're storing the information with how you'll feel when you have to retrieve it. If you learn something when you're tired and surrounded by noise, you'll have trouble recalling it at test time, when it's quiet and you're alert.

Memory's Strange Roots

Ancient Chinese emperors used to eat ginseng root in the belief that it made their brains work better. New evidence shows that they were right. Ginseng contains something that improves the biochemical reaction in the brain that is believed to be linked to memory.

BRAIN BENDER
How many questions
can you think of that will
give the answer
GREEN?

• • •

Memories Can Lie

Researchers now know that one in three people can be fooled into remembering childhood events that never happened. In one experiment, volunteers were shown fake Disneyland advertisements featuring Bugs Bunny — a Warner Brothers cartoon character who definitely would never be seen at Disneyland! When quizzed later, a third of the volunteers remembered meeting Bugs Bunny during childhood visits to Disneyland and some even recollected stroking his ears!

Police also know that a "false memory" like this can be surprisingly easy to create. A report of criminals escaping in a white van, for instance, might trigger false memories in eyewitnesses of a white van leaving the scene of the crime, even though the actual getaway vehicle was a blue car.

What's Your Earliest Memory?

How far back can you remember? You probably can't remember much before you were about three years old. Why?

By the time you were two years old, you were experiencing two basic types of memories. The first would be general — the color of the walls in your room, or your favorite foods. The second took care of specific events, such as a trip to the zoo. After your third birthday, you began to develop the ability to pick and choose events from the second kind of memory and weave them together to form a long-term memory of your life.

What happened to you between the ages of two and four? Most importantly, you learned to speak. And your parents were teaching you how to tell stories . . . memories are often stored as little stories. Until you could make up your own stories about things you did or things that happened to you, you couldn't file your memories away in that form. And since these things were not stored in long-term memory, they are not available for you to recall them years later.

THINKING

WELCOME TO PARTS OF YOUR BRAIN THAT ARE IN SOME WAYS uniquely human. You're going to get to know the superhero of your brain — your cortex. Your cortex sets your brain apart from the brains of other animals. It's the outer surface of your brain, and it's full of folds and crevices so that you can pack more brain into a small space.

You do most of your thinking with your cortex. You're using it now to read these words. And it does all your imagining too. Try this: imagine a rhinoceros in your kitchen — right there by the fridge. Everything about your mental image of that rhino — its size, color, smell, the grunts it makes — was put together in your cortex.

And that's not all. Your right cortex is different from your left. A boy's cortex is different from a girl's. And your brain is different from everyone else's. Sometimes your cortex even creates its own stories — they're called dreams.

So enjoy this last part of the trip: you and your brain should have fun doing it.

TWO BRAINS IN ONE

BACK IN THE EARLY 1800S, PEOPLE BELIEVED THAT THE BUMPS on your skull could reveal what sort of person you were. You could even go to an expert, called a phrenologist, who would feel your head bumps and say something like, "You are very careful and keep your room neat . . . and you have a particularly well-developed bump of humor."

Sideways Glances

Ask someone to solve the Brain Bender below and watch which way their eyes look while they're thinking.

Some scientists have suggested that if a person looks to the left, the right side of the brain is being used to solve the puzzle. A glance to the right means the work is being done by the left side of the brain.

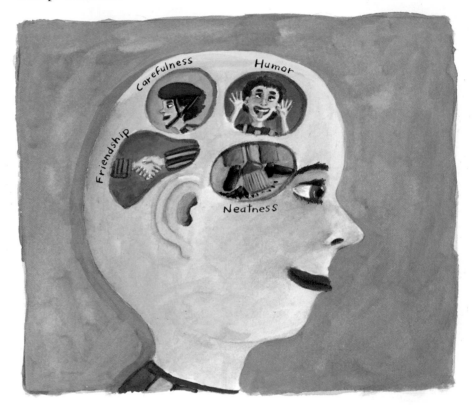

BRAIN BENDER
In which contest do the winners move backwards and the losers move forwards?

• • •

The idea behind phrenology was that each character trait had its own place on the surface of the brain. Nobody takes any of this seriously today, but brain scientists do agree that the brain has many different parts, and those parts have different responsibilities. One of the most important things discovered in mapping the brain is the difference between the right side of your brain and the left.

Right Brain, Left Brain

Did you know that each half of your brain controls the opposite side of your body? The right half of your brain controls the movements of your left arm and leg. It receives messages from them and the rest of your left side. The opposite is true for the left half of your brain.

Words and Pictures

Your right and left brains even think in different ways. For example, your left brain contains the main control centers for speech, while your right brain seems to be better at figuring out three-dimensional problems.

Some of these puzzles will give your right brain a workout, some will do the same for your left. (Answers on page 63.)

Right-Brain Workout

1. There are three spots on this folded piece of paper. Are all three spots on the same side of the paper?

2. Which two of these puzzle pieces fit together to form a square?

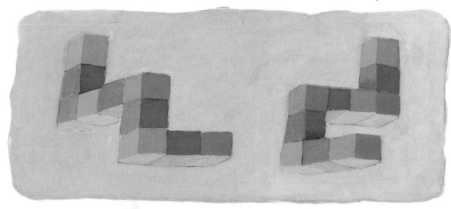

3. Turn these three-dimensional figures in your mind and decide if they're identical.

Try this

Look at the letters below and decide, as fast as you can, which of them are written normally and which are backwards. (Answers on page 63.) You'll find that it takes you longer to figure out the letters that are upside-down. That's because you have to turn them around *in your mind* before you can see whether they're the right way 'round or not. That turning seems to be done mostly in your right brain.

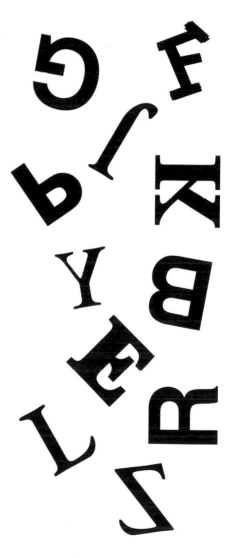

Rockabye Baby

Why does a mother cradle her baby so that its head is on her left? It used to be thought that a mother did this so that her baby could hear her heartbeat more easily. But here's a more recent suggestion. If the baby's face is on the mother's left, then a glance sends the image of the baby's face to the mother's right brain. Because this side of her brain is better at recognizing emotions, the mother can respond more quickly if she sees an unhappy baby.

Left-Brain Workout

1. Five girls ran a race. Michelle finished before Rachel, but behind Sara. Lucia finished before Kim but behind Rachel. In what order did they finish the race?

2. Three boxes in your kitchen cupboard are labeled "nuts," "raisins" and "nuts and raisins," but all the labels are wrong and you have to correct them. The catch — you cannot peek inside any of the boxes and you may select only one item from one box to help you decide what's inside all the boxes.

3. Two of the biggest spotted dogs you ever saw have a total of 86 spots between them. One has 10 more spots than the other. How many spots does each dog have?

Happy Faces

Look quickly at the noses of the two faces to the left. Now make a fast decision: which face looks happier to you?

Four out of five people choose the bottom face, but if you look closely you'll see that the two faces are just mirror images of each other! So why do most people think the bottom face is happier? Scientists suspect that your right brain makes the decision for you.

Because you looked at the noses, your right brain saw the left half of each picture (through the left half of your eyes) while your left brain saw the right half (through the right half of your eyes). To see what your right brain saw at a glance, cover up the right half of both pictures. What do you see? A happy face below and a sad face above. Because your right brain saw the mouth curling up on the left half of the bottom picture, and because it is faster and better at seeing emotions than your left brain, that's the face you most likely picked. (However, if you're left-handed, you might have picked the other one.)

Make a Face for Science

Psychologists at the University of Toronto have found that you can cause either side of your brain to produce the emotions that they control. How? Just by moving your mouth!

The psychologists' findings suggest that people tend to feel sad after they put on a left-sided smile, and "good" or "up" after putting on a right-sided smile. This experiment seems to show that when the right brain goes into action to move the facial muscles on the left side, it also expresses its emotions, which are generally unhappy. The opposite is true for the left brain. Do you agree?

Try this

Use your face muscles to lift just the left side of your mouth and hold it for a minute or so. Do you feel any different emotionally?

Now repeat the experiment, putting on a right-sided smile. How do you feel after a minute or so?

Two Halves Make a Whole

All these stories about the differences between the two sides of your brain are fascinating, but there's one thing you should never forget. Even though your right and left brains are better at different things, they are constantly talking to each other. They *never* work alone. So it's impossible to use just the right side of your brain when you're doing puzzles, or just your left brain when you're writing a letter. You always use your whole brain.

TALK, TALK, TALK!

HAVE YOU EVER WONDERED WHAT GOES ON IN YOUR BRAIN when you talk to a friend? Is there some sort of dictionary in your brain? Where do all those words come from?

Bright Ideas

These brain scans show what happens when the brain works with words. The bright areas in the pictures are places where there's a sudden increase in blood flow, which might be needed to supply oxygen to brain cells that have suddenly become active. In these pictures you're looking at the left side of someone's brain.

Peel Me a Whatchamacallit

Sometimes the victim of a brain injury turns out to be a big help to scientists who are trying to understand what your brain does when you talk. A few years ago a Boston man suffered a slight stroke, which caused him an amazing memory problem. If the doctors showed him pictures of cars, musical instruments and most other objects, he had no trouble naming them. But with pictures of fruits or vegetables, he'd either give the wrong name or couldn't name it at all.

Does this mean that your brain looks a bit like a supermarket on the inside, with all the names for fruits and veggies in one place? This case, and others like it, suggest that we store words for similar things in the same place in the brain.

In the scan on the left, areas at the back of the brain become active when a person sees a word — such as cake.

The scan to the right shows the brain at work when the person is asked to repeat the same word out loud.

Completely different areas of the brain become active when the same person is asked to think of an action word, or verb, that goes with cake *— such as* eat *or* bake.

The small round yellow spot you see in the bottom picture shows up bright only the first few times a person is asked to think of a verb. After that, it stops lighting up. It seems the more often your brain has to do something the less it has to work at it.

Find the Right Words

Scientists have known for more than 100 years that the left side of the brain is the "language" side. But the research that gave us the brain scans opposite also revealed that the right side of the brain is at work in word tests. It may be that both sides are at work, but doing different things.

The left brain *is* the side that puts sentences together when you're about to speak, or takes them apart so you can understand them. But the words in those sentences might come from anywhere in your brain: from the right side or even, surprisingly, from the cerebellum, the back part of your brain that controls and coordinates movements.

On the Tip of My Tongue!

The next time you are struggling to remember a word that you're sure you know, you might be able to get clues to how that word is stored in your brain. What can you remember about it? You usually have a good idea how long the word is, and even what its first and last syllables are. But the middle of the word seems lost. Scientists call this the "bathtub effect." They imagine the word as a very tall person in a bathtub. Her head and feet stick up, but her middle is submerged in the tub!

BRAIN BENDER
Can you turn the word LOSE into FIND in four steps? Change only one letter at a time and create a new word in each step.

L O S E

F I N D

51

Girls 'n' Boys

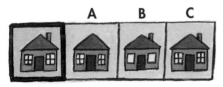

A   B   C

1. Which of the three houses on the right is identical to the one on the left?

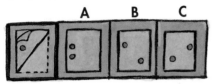

A   B   C

2. When the piece of paper on the left is unfolded, which piece shows where the holes will fall?

3. Find as many synonyms (words that mean the same thing) for the following words as you can in three minutes:

clear   dark   strong   wild

A   B   C

4. The shape on the left, above, is hidden in one of the three boxes. But which box is it?

EVERYONE KNOWS THAT BOYS AND GIRLS ARE DIFFERENT. THEIR scores on certain tests suggest that there may be differences between girls' and boys' brains. But whether the difference is found in the brain or is caused by other things — like how boys and girls are raised — is a complicated puzzle that may never be untangled!

Try this
Do the puzzles at left. Turn to page 63 for the answers, and to find out which ones are usually done better by girls and which by boys.

Remember When?

Some scientists have even suggested that some differences between girls and boys can be traced back to a time tens or even hundreds of thousands of years ago. Back when our ancestors were hunter-gatherers, it's thought that the men got together and went off to hunt, while the women stayed closer to home, taking care of the children and gathering insect grubs, roots and plants. Does your brain retain a permanent record of this ancient way of life?

Try this
Take exactly one minute to familiarize yourself with all the objects in this picture, then cover it up.

Here's a picture of the same objects, but some of them have been moved. Which ones? Make a list of the things you think have been moved. Take your time. When you're finished, uncover the first picture and see how well you did.

BRAIN BENDER
An Australian aborigine can throw a boomerang so that it can return without bouncing off anything. How can you do the same with a tennis ball?

When adults do this puzzle, women usually do better than men. One of the explanations for this might be that long ago, women had to be very good at remembering the exact places where things like the juiciest roots could be found. But locating things that didn't move couldn't help men hunt fast-moving animals!

Psychologists at the University of Rochester discovered that male and female students also use different ways of finding their way through mazes. Most of the boys relied on what's called dead reckoning: "I'll go straight for a while, turn left, then go about twice as far." Do you suppose that this was a better strategy for hunting animals thousands of years ago? The girls usually used landmarks instead: "Turn left at the billboard with the big hamburger on it, then go straight until you see the tree with the balloon caught in its branches."

Keep an Open Mind

Tests and experiments like the ones here only predict *on average* who will do better, boys or girls. And the causes for the differences remain a mystery — the idea that our hunter-gatherer past causes them is just a guess. Always keep in mind that every kid should be judged individually on what he or she can do, not on what he or she is supposed to be able to do.

Amaze-ing Rats

Research with rats in mazes reveals that male and female rats differ in finding their way the same way that we do. Female rats seemed to use "landmarks" such as marks on the maze walls to find their way through. Male rats were much better than females at running through mazes where landmarks had been removed. Can these differences in navigating be traced to ancient hunting and gathering practices? Not likely, since ancient rats weren't out killing mammoths or gathering berries like our human ancestors.

MUSCLE HEADS

IT IS OFTEN SAID THAT YOU USE ONLY TEN PERCENT OF YOUR brain, but brain scientists say that's not true. There are no big, empty spaces in your brain just waiting to be filled. You're actually using almost all your brain all the time. But even so, there are hints that you might be able to use your brain more efficiently than you already do. All you have to do is exercise it!

Practice Makes . . . Smart!

A California scientist has found that the smarter you get, the less your brain needs to work. He used a brain imaging machine to watch what happened as one group of people played a video game while another group just watched numbers flashing on a screen. As you'd expect, the game players' brains worked harder. But only at first. After a month or two of practice, their brains weren't burning energy nearly as fast as at the start of the experiment. In fact, their brains weren't even working as hard as those of the people who were idly watching numbers. This amazing result suggests that, like muscles, your brain can learn to do things more efficiently with enough practice.

The colors in these pictures show brain activity, with the areas of most activity appearing bright orange and yellow. The picture on the left shows the brain of someone playing a video game. The picture on the right shows the same person playing the same video game after a lot of practice. Notice how small the orange areas became.

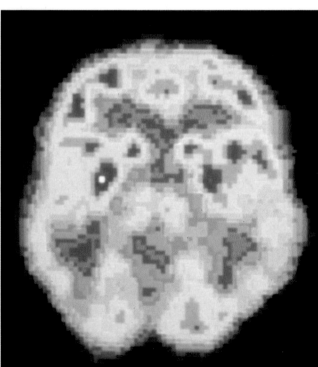
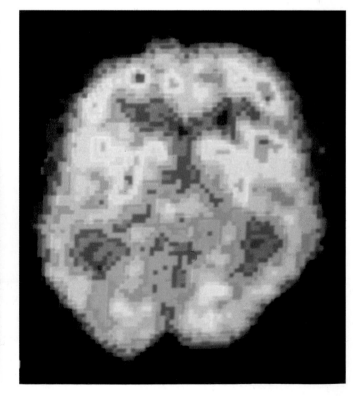

Double Trouble

Practice increases brain efficiency, but can it help it do two things at one time?

Try these

- Rub one hand in circles on your stomach while you pat your head with the other. It's tricky, but with practice it gets easier. What happens if you swap hands?

- Try to tap on a table three times in a steady beat with your right hand in the same time it takes you to tap twice in a steady beat with your left hand. This one's more difficult, isn't it?

Some scientists believe that you find it hard to do two different things at the same time because you're using the same, or neighboring, parts of your brain for both things.

Do the Stroop

One of the best ways to prove how difficult it is to do two things at the same time is the Stroop Test, named after J. Ridley Stroop, who invented it in the 1930s. Look at the words in colors to the right. Now name, out loud, the colors *in which the words are printed.*

Funny, isn't it? It takes real concentration to say the color that the word is printed in and to ignore the word that you see at the same time. Why? It could be simply that reading is something you do much more than naming colors. When your brain sees a word and a color at the same time, it tries to read the word even though it's supposed to be naming the color.

Try this

Be the champion of double think. Get two books — one you would like to read, and one a young reader would enjoy. Ask a friend to read to you from the simpler of the books and write down what she says. Here's the difficult part — continue to write down what you hear and at the same time read your own book. To make sure you're not faking it, your friend can quiz you later on what you read from your book.

Don't get too discouraged if you can't do this at first. It can take weeks to learn how. But it is possible to understand and remember different things you read and write at the same time!

YELLOW

RED

BLUE

GREEN

PURPLE

BLACK

IN YOUR DREAMS

DREAMS ARE THE WEIRDEST EVENTS THAT GO ON IN YOUR BRAIN. Most of your dreams happen during a kind of sleep known as REM, which stands for *rapid eye movement*. It's called that because your eyes move back and forth while it is going on. But your eyes are about the only things that move while you're dreaming. During REM sleep your arms and legs are paralyzed! In fact, dreaming is so mysterious that scientists can't agree on why you dream.

Dreamless Sleep

There are two very curious things about the echidna, or spiny anteater. It never has REM sleep, and it has a huge brain for its size.

Do a big brain and the lack of REM sleep have anything to do with each other? The answer may be "yes" if dreams get rid of useless information in a process of "unlearning." Does the echidna need a very big brain to store the information it can't unlearn by dreaming? If so, just think how big your brain would have to be if you didn't have REM sleep . . . you'd have to wear a neck brace to hold up your extra-heavy head.

Mysterious Dreams

Some scientists think dreams are brain trash — scraps of information dumped so there's room for more information the next day. According to this theory, dreams aren't worth remembering, since they're just nonsensical pieces of your brain's busy day.

Others think dreams are just the opposite of trash: they are the highlights of your brain's day, which are recorded at night when it can devote more attention to this important task. You don't have to remember your dreams because they create a record of important brain events in your long-term memory.

Still others think that your brain makes up dream stories to explain all the strange and unconnected images it produces during sleep. Or that dreaming is like an aerobics class for your brain, working out the most important circuits of nerves. But whatever the answer, dreams must be important, or you wouldn't have them several times a night.

Lucid Dreaming

It's possible to control what happens in your dreams. All you have to do is learn how to do something called lucid dreaming.

Imagine you're dreaming that you're flying over your neighborhood. With practice you might be able to decide in the middle of your dream to swoop down low, then fly up into the clouds, even hover over the park where your friends are playing. The key to lucid dreaming is recognizing when you are in a dream.

Dream Master

Several times a day ask yourself, "Am I dreaming?" Each time, even though you're absolutely sure you are awake, check carefully. Make sure everything is as it should be. Are shadows where they ought to be? Is the sky the right color?

This sounds silly, but there's a good reason for doing it. Once this "reality check" becomes a habit, someday you just might do it when you're dreaming. You'll suddenly realize you're in the middle of a dream, and then you can try to make things happen. Have you ever had a really scary nightmare of a monster and woken up from it shaking and in a sweat? If you were a lucid dreamer, you might be able to scare away the monster instead of waking up terrified.

Don't be discouraged if you don't become a lucid dreamer right away. The more you think about it and the longer you work at it, the better your chances are of succeeding.

Dream Phantoms

Imagine you're having a lucid dream: the surroundings are strange, but you're not worried because you know you're in a dream. A ghost suddenly appears — but you just laugh to yourself and say, "It's only a dream."

But what if you slipped into a dream while you were awake? If you thought you were awake and a ghost suddenly appeared, you'd be scared out of your wits. Maybe this is what happens when people see mysterious things like ghosts and UFOs.

One clue that supports this idea is that ghost and UFO sightings are often accompanied by changes in the entire scene . . . changes in the light or the temperature or the color of the sky. One way to explain this kind of change is to suppose that the person slipped, unknowingly, into a waking dream. So are ghosts and UFOs waking dreams? We may never know for sure.

Try this
This puzzle seems nightmarish, yet its solution isn't scary at all. Don't go to page 63 if it stumps you. Think of it at bedtime, and you might dream the answer!

Jonathan was running home. He was almost there when he met a masked man holding an object that scared him. Jonathan turned in panic and ran back to where he came from. The man chased Jonathan and threw the object at him. What's happening here?

Puzzling Dreams

Did you know that some people have used their dreams to solve puzzles that stumped them when they were awake? Writers, poets, inventors, composers, politicians, archaeologists, scientists — even brain and dream researchers — have cited their dreams as a source of inspiration and creative thinking. A famous sleep researcher, Dr. William Dement, wondered if dreams could help us solve problems. He gave students brain-bending puzzles to work out 15 minutes before they went to sleep. Here's one of the problems he used. (Answer below.)

Try this
These letters are the first five in a sequence: O, T, T, F, F. What should the next two letters be?

Dream On
The latest research into dreams seems to show a surprising thing: the time you spend asleep just might be nonstop dream time. Instead of doing most of our dreaming in REM sleep, we might be very close to a dream state even when we're awake! So whatever you do, don't forget to keep asking yourself, "Am I awake or am I dreaming?"

The puzzle works like this: These are the first letters in the words *one, two, three, four, five*. Therefore the next two letters are S (*six*) and S (*seven*). One student who was given this puzzle dreamed of being in an art gallery looking at paintings. In the dream, the student counted the paintings — one, two, three, four, five. But the sixth and seventh paintings had been ripped from their frames and were missing! The student realized that the sixth and seventh spaces were the key to the solution of the puzzle.

Dr. Dement's experiment wasn't a success, since there were only a few dream solutions out of 1,148 attempts by 500 students. But even those few hint at the possible power of dreams.

LAST THOUGHTS

REMEMBER THE NONSENSE RHYME FROM PAGE 37? CAN YOU retrieve it from your long-term memory and recite it out loud? Of course you can! After the workout you've given your brain by reading this book, it's in peak form. Brain power is a bit like muscle strength: the more you use it, the more efficient it gets. And if you don't use it, you'll lose it!

You've almost finished your amazing journey through the brain. But the adventure is far from over. Some of the discoveries you've read about in this book are truly remarkable, but many more are sure to follow. Maybe in the future brain experts will learn how to make a blind person see. They might come up with surefire ways of developing an extraordinary memory. Who knows? One day scientists might be able to look at your brain waves and be able to guess what you're thinking about.

But there is a long way to go. We know a great deal about some things in the brain, but very little about others. For example, scientists are just now beginning to figure out what happens in your brain when you do something as simple as reach for your sandwich at lunch! There are still many mysteries and unanswered questions about the incredible pink stuff between your ears.

USER'S GUIDE TO THE BRAIN

Your brain can be divided into four main parts, with each part being responsible for specific jobs.

hippocampus

amygdalas

Your **feeling brain**, made up of your **limbic system**, which includes your **hippocampus** and **amygdalas**, plays a big role in your emotions and laying down memory.

Your **thinking brain** is made up of your **cerebrum** (which means *not-so-little brain*). It receives messages from your senses and interprets the world through them, stores memories, and allows you to understand, communicate and express emotions.

Your **cerebellum** (which means *little brain*) acts like a small computer to coordinate information from your cerebrum and your muscles so that you can do things like walk, ride a bike or play soccer. It also gives you the ability to know the position of any part of your body without seeing it and, as we've recently discovered, is involved in some kinds of memory and language.

brainstem

pons

medulla

Your **reptilian brain**, made up of your **brainstem**, **medulla** and **pons**, takes care of the things you never have to think about, such as your heart beat, digestion, breathing sneezing, and coughing.

Your thinking brain, or cerebrum, up close

Your cerebrum is made up of two halves, known as **hemispheres**.

The crinkly surface of your cerebrum is known as the cerebral **cortex** (which means *bark*). The cortex consists of six layers of cells. It is here that you do most of your thinking.

The **left cerebral hemisphere** is *mostly* responsible for speech, reasoning, reading, writing and arithmetic.

Both halves of your cerebrum are connected by bundles of nerve fibers, the most important being the **corpus callosum**.

The **right cerebral hemisphere** is *mostly* responsible for awareness of three-dimensional forms, appreciation of music and art, insight, imagination and creativity.

A quick tour around your thinking brain

Just about everything you can see when you look at a human brain is the thinking brain, or cerebrum. It evolved most recently, and covers the older parts of the brain. Your cerebrum is divided into several **lobes** by deep folds known as **sulci** (which means *furrows*). The view at right is from the top, with the front of the brain in green.

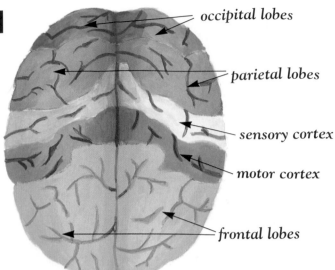

occipital lobes

parietal lobes

sensory cortex

motor cortex

frontal lobes

Frontal lobes (left and right) contain your olfactory (smell) centers and handle working memory, reasoning, planning, some language and — with your feeling brain — your emotions.

The **motor cortex** (spanning both cerebral hemispheres) is the home of your movement "kidunculus" and tells your muscles when to move.

The **sensory cortex** (spanning both cerebral hemispheres) is the home of your "kidunculus" touch map, and processes information from your sense of touch.

Parietal lobes (left and right) receive information from all your senses.

front

back

Temporal lobes (left and right) contain your major speech and language centers (on the left), and handle face recognition (mostly on the right), some memory and hearing.

Occipital lobes (left and right) handle what you see and how you interpret it.

Answers

Senses

Page 15 • ***Uncommon Scents:*** 1 – C, leafcutter ants;
2 – **A**, silkworm moth (male uses feathery antennae to pick up female scent);
3 – **B**, honeybees with queen bee.

Page 17 • ***Try this:*** The section at the tip of the tongue is most sensitive to sweet tastes. The sections along the sides of the tongue overlap salt- and sour-sensitive areas.

Brain Benders

Page 8 • There are twelve 2-cent stamps in a dozen.
Page 10 • Once upon a time
Page 13 • The beanstalk was 10 m (33 ft.) high on the ninth day.
Page 16 • Five slices of chocolate cake were eaten.
Page 20 • The man was bald.
Page 22 • Neither is heavier — both weigh 1 kg.

Emotions

Page 25 • ***Phobia Name Game:*** 1 – C, 2 – E, 3 – A, 4 – F, 5 – D, 6 – G, 7 – B.
Page 28 • ***Try this:*** 1 – anger, 2 – happiness, 3 – sadness, 4 – surprise, 5 – disgust, 6 – fear.
Page 29 • ***To Tell the Truth:*** The kid on the top broke the vase.
Page 30 • ***Body Talk:*** 1. "I'm totally bored and don't want to listen to anything you say."
2. "You are making me feel uncomfortable because you're sitting too close."
3. "I'm really nervous."
4. "I find you really attractive and if you'd like to get to know me better, that's okay."
Page 31 • ***Sign Language:*** In southern Italy, nodding the head up and down and saying "tssskk" means *no*; in Russia, nodding the head up and down means *yes*. In Spain, an up-and-down wave of the hand with the palm facing the ground means *come here*; in Australia, the same gesture means *goodbye*. In southern India, shaking the head back and forth means *yes*; in Germany, the same gesture means *no*.
Page 32 • ***Fuzzy Feelings:*** The lion-tailed macaque on the left is showing a "fear grin" — an instinctive submissive expression; the mandrill in the center is displaying aggression; the orangutan on the right looks bored.

Brain Benders

Page 24 • CDFG is the odd one out because, although its letters are in alphabetical order, they are not in consecutive order — the letter E is missing between D and F.
Page 31 • The man wasn't arrested because he was walking.
Page 32 • John has three pets.

Memory

Page 42 • ***Try this:*** Designs 2, 5, 6, 7, 9 and 11 are repeated from page 40.

Brain Benders

Page 34 • If you saw the combination WXY 9, you'd be looking at the number 9 touch pad on a telephone.
Page 39 • All of the months of the year have 28 days.
• The months in alphabetical order are April, August, December, February, January, July, June, March, May, November, October, September.

Thinking

Page 47 • ***Right-Brain Workout:*** **1.** No, two spots are on one side, one on the other; **2.** The blue pieces form a square; **3.** They're identical.
• ***Try this:*** The letters G, F, J, B, E, L and R are written normally. The P, K, Y and Z are backwards.
Page 48 • ***Left-Brain Workout:*** **1.** They finished the race in this order: Sara, Michelle, Rachel, Lucia and Kim.
2. Take an item from the box marked "nuts and raisins," and switch that label with the label for whatever is in your hand. Then switch the other two labels.
3. One has 48 spots, the other has 38.
Page 52 • ***Try this:*** **1.** C, girls; **2.** B, boys; **3.** girls average 4.1 per word, boys average 2.2 per word; **4.** B, boys.
Page 58 • ***Try this:*** Jonathan is playing baseball. The masked man is the catcher and the object he's about to throw is a baseball.

Brain Benders

Page 46 • Tug-of-war
Page 51 • LOSE/LONE/LINE/FINE/FIND
Page 53 • Throw the ball straight up into the air.

Index